BERLIT

LOS ANGELES

- A V in the text denotes a highly recommended sight
- A complete A–Z of practical information starts on p.115
- Extensive mapping throughout: on cover flaps and in text

Printed in Switzerland by Weber SA, Bienne.

1st edition (1995/1996)

Although we make every effort to ensure the accuracy of the information in this guide, changes do occur. If you have any new information, suggestions or corrections to contribute to the guide, we would like to hear from you. Please write to Berlitz Publishing at one of the above addresses.

Text:	Donna Dailey
Editors:	Delphine Verroest, Hazel Clarke
Photography:	All photographs by Donna Dailey, except pp.14, 25, 29, 33, 37, 42, 45, 58, 60, 64, 82, 101, 104, 107, 112, 114 by Doug Traverso, and p.99 kindly supplied by Los Angeles Visitors and Convention Bureau.
Layout:	Suzanna Boyle
Cartography:	Visual Image
Thanks to:	Los Angeles Convention and Visitors Bureau for their invaluable assistance in the preparation of this guide.

Cover photographs: Front: *Los Angeles city view towards San Gabriel Mountains* © Tony Stone Worldwide
Back: *Do Woop singers*

CONTENTS

Los Angeles and its People

No other city in the world during this century has captured people's hopes and imaginations more than Los Angeles. It has replaced New York as the immigration gateway to the United States, and for Americans, to whom the West has always symbolized new beginnings and a chance to reinvent oneself, there is nowhere more 'west' than L.A. To everyone else, however, it's the *wunderkind* of popular culture, fame and fortune in the fast lane.

Perhaps it's the intoxicating mix of beaches, blue skies and palm trees that fosters the belief that in L.A., anything can happen. Somewhere along the line, the city that was christened the Queen of the Angels became the Queen of Dreams.

Invincible Spirit

People have always come here for the climate. Situated in a fertile basin edged by mountains and the sea, blessed with mild temperatures and year-round sunshine, Southern California does indeed seem like God's little paradise. It was the climate that lured the industrious farmers of the Midwest, who by the mid-1930s turned this Garden of Eden into the most prosperous agricultural region in the country. The climate also brought in the movie people, who even now shape L.A.'s fortunes and the *zeitgeist* of the Western world; and the climate lures about 25 million tourists a year.

From its inception, Los Angeles has been characterized by its invincibile spirit. This inland town transformed a shallow, unprotected bay into one of the great ports of the world, and it was through determined self-promotion that Los Angeles grew from a sleepy Spanish pueblo into the second largest city in the United States.

Business-wise, L.A. is the capital city of the Pacific Rim. It is the West Coast's leading financial centre, and is second only to New York in its volume of retail trade. Although **5**

Theme parks such as this one at Universal Studios are always an irresistible draw for families.

the 1960s, a municipal ordinance restricted buildings to 13 storeys in height. This was due partly to fear of earthquakes, and partly to a feeling of unlimited space to expand. Today, as the city's population is approaching 3.5 million, the latter no longer applies. Modern skyscrapers are built on hydraulic rollers designed so that the buildings roll, rather than shake, during a quake, and L.A. boasts the tallest building west of Chicago – the 73-storey First Interstate World Center. Another boost to downtown growth was the $485 million expansion, completed in 1993, of the Los Angeles Convention Center, which is the largest such facility on the West Coast.

entertainment is its biggest industry, it also ranks among the largest manufacturing areas in the country, particularly in the fields of aerospace and engineering, and is one of the country's major oil-refining centres.

However, downtown L.A.'s skyline was a late bloomer and only began in recent years to **6** reflect the city's success. Until

Dream Capital

L.A. has a chameleon-like ability to be many things to many people. Some come here for business, some for the beaches, some for the spectacular theme parks. Disneyland, Hollywood, Venice Beach, Sunset Boulevard ... such names evoke more than just the places themselves.

L.A. is simply the sum of a vast number of eclectic parts. Within its boundaries there are 88 separate, incorporated cities, many of which have their own city halls, police forces and fire brigades. The city as a whole also has the curious tendency to spawn new cities, inwardly as well as on its fringes.

The result is that L.A. is a city with no heart, geographically speaking, but with lots of soul. You'll hear Spanish (and other languages) being spoken as frequently as you'll hear English. There are large Chinese, African-American, Korean and Japanese communities in the city (indeed, L.A. has the country's second largest Asian population behind Honolulu), while Hispanics are the largest ethnic group, with their

Destroyed by fire in 1986, the restored Central Library rises like a phoenix in downtown L.A.

numbers fast approaching 40 percent of the population.

Car Culture

Although L.A. is notorious for its freeway traffic, the thought of driving is actually more intimidating than the act itself. Streets and highway exits are well marked, and most streets are on a grid – so that if you do miss a turn, you can simply go around the block and try again.

The nation's 10 busiest freeways are all in the L.A. vicinity, including Highway 101, the busiest of them all, which handles half a million cars every day. If you drive along Sunset or Wilshire Boulevards from downtown to the sea, you will see a cross-section of L.A. cultures in 16 short miles (25km).

To combat highway congestion and pollution, L.A. is now building a much needed public transport network. Downtown and Long Beach were connected by light rail in 1990, and the first leg of the new subway line opened in 1993.

Strict emission controls for cars and industry have considerably reduced L.A.'s notorious smog, but air quality can be poor. What is often mistaken for smog is actually the marine layer, a thick, grey bank of low-lying cloud that drifts in from the ocean in June and early July. This can cause visitors much distress, if they expect California sunshine every day. Luckily, the cloud usually burns off by mid-day.

L.A. Today

Los Angeles in the early 1990s had more than its fair share of troubles, including race riots in spring 1992 following the Rodney King trial (see p.21).

The riots underscored the social problems that fester beneath the surface of the city. Much of the violence coming out of the black ghettoes of south-central L.A. was aimed against the Asian minorities. Some businesses managed to recover fast, but others never will, and an uneasiness lingers in many Asian communities.

Despite racial tensions and dwindling resources for social services, L.A. is still a mecca for immigrants, in particular from Mexico. Illegal immigration is a smouldering issue here. Los Angeles also has the USA's largest homeless population, who you will see everywhere: in parks, on off-ramps of freeways, even on the polished streets of Beverly Hills.

In the fall of 1993, forest fires raged through the western mountains and down into Malibu, destroying many luxurious homes. With the arrival of winter, flooding and mudslides brought further damage. Then in January 1994 an earthquake measuring 6.6 on the Richter scale struck the San Fernando Valley, bringing down several sections of the L.A. freeways. Thousands were left homeless in the Valley, but downtown L.A., the Westside and a considerable number of attractions and hotels were spared any serious damage, and repairs were soon underway to rebuild the main traffic arteries.

As visitors, L.A. will mostly strike you as a place in which to be amused and amazed. Angelenos are generally friendly and helpful, and in a city of aspiring stars, everyday encounters can provide a good show.

You won't be able to experience all of L.A. in one visit. With its climate, variety and exuberance, Los Angeles is seductive. In 1921, the All-Year Club was founded to attract tourists to Southern California, hopefully to stay permanently. They estimated that one out of every ten visitors comes back to live. You have been warned. **9**

A Brief History

While the Spanish conquistadors scoured the New World for the gold of popular legend, the untouched wealth of California lay right under their noses. In 1542, some 23 years after Cortez vanquished Mexico, Juan Rodriguez Cabrillo, a Portuguese navigator in the service of King Charles I of Spain, sailed north to explore the Pacific coast and discovered San Pedro Bay, just south of Los Angeles. He named it Bahia de los Fumos (Bay of the Smokes) because of the many Indian campfires which he saw along the shore.

Before the Spanish arrived, California was home to more Indians per square mile than any other part of what is now the United States. There is evidence that they were a healthy people, suffering little blindness or chronic disease. They had no immunity to European illnesses however, and when the Spanish arrived hundreds died from chickenpox, measles and venereal diseases.

For two centuries, L.A. was nothing more than a pit stop on the trans-Pacific naval highway – a convenient refuelling place for Spanish galleons on their way back to Mexico from the Philippines.

In the meantime, other nations were casting their eyes on California. The Englishman Sir Francis Drake had landed on shore to claim it for the Queen; the French had just acquired a good chunk of America from the Mississippi to the Rockies; and Russians from the Bering Sea were hunting sea otters, whose pelts would fetch $100 apiece in the Orient. To strengthen its claim to the region, Spain decided to colonize 'Alta California'.

The Founding of Los Angeles

The mission they established played an important role in the growth of the Spanish empire, helping to consolidate colonial territories and extend borders. While other parts of America were settled in spite of the Indians, California was settled

HISTORICAL LANDMARKS

1771 Founding of Mission San Gabriel Arcangel.

1781 Founding of El Pueblo de Nuestra Señora la Reina de Los Angeles de Porciúncula.

1825 California becomes a territory of Mexico.

1848 Treaty of Guadalupe Hidalgo ends the Mexican-American War. California becomes part of the United States.

1850 California becomes a state.

1853 Don Matteo Keeler plants the first orange trees.

1876 The first transcontinental railroad, the Southern Pacific, arrives in Los Angeles.

1880 The University of Southern California is founded.

1881 The *Los Angeles Times* publishes its first issue.

1892 Oil is discovered in downtown Los Angeles.

1902 The first movie house, the Electric Theatre, opens.

1909 Santa Monica Pier is erected.

1913 Cecil B DeMille makes the first full-length feature film, *The Squaw Man*, in a barn near Selma and Vine.

1923 The Hollywood sign is erected.

1927 Graumann's Chinese Theatre (now Mann's) opens. The Academy of Motion Picture Arts & Sciences is founded at the Biltmore Hotel.

1928 L.A.'s first airport, called 'Mines Field', opens on the site of the current LAX.

1932 The 1932 Summer Olympics take place in L.A.

1947 Hollywood Freeway links L.A. with San Fernando Valley.

1955 Disneyland opens in Anaheim.

1961 Hollywood's Walk of Fame is launched.

1980 US census puts population of Los Angeles and Orange County area at 10 million.

1984 The XXIII Olympiad is held in L.A.

1990 L.A.'s first light rail transit line opens.

1994 An earthquake measuring 6.6 on the Richter scale rocks the San Fernando Valley.

Life at the Missions

The padres faced many hardships in establishing California's chain of missions. Isolated from other outposts and their base in Mexico, they suffered from insufficient supplies, starvation, disease and occasional hostile attacks by Indians.

When building the missions, the padres copied the style familiar to them in their native Spain. The typical structure was a large, rambling building, with four sides surrounding a central square. The largest and most impressive building was always the church, which was decorated with the best materials that could be obtained from the old country.

The padres befriended the natives by offering them gifts of bright beads, food and clothing. Once the Indians had agreed to join the mission community, they could never again leave without permission. They were well fed, however, and the monotony of work and prayer was relieved by the frequent celebration of feast days with processions, fiestas and games.

Three of the original 21 missions still stand in the Los Angeles area. Mission San Fernando Rey de España in the San Fernando Valley and Mission San Juan Capistrano in Orange County have been restored and give a fine portrayal of mission life. Even though Mission San Gabriel Arcangel in the San Gabriel Valley was heavily damaged in an earthquake in 1988, the grounds are still open to the public.

because of them. Spain had already made headway in setting up missions throughout Mexico, and was now determined to bring Christianity to the Native Americans.

In 1769 an expedition led by Father Junípero Serra, a 55-year-old Franciscan priest, and Captain Gaspar de Portolá set forth, and at the end of a gruelling journey arrived in what is now San Diego. There, Father Serra founded the first of a chain of 21 missions that was to stretch up the coast to San Francisco. The route that ran between them was known as

El Camino Real (the King's Highway) and it roughly parallelled today's California State Highway 1.

From San Diego, Captain Portolá went north to Monterey, stopping on the way at 'a delightful place among the trees on the river' in order to trade trinkets with local Indians. This site was to become the birthplace of Los Angeles.

Mission San Gabriel Arcangel, founded in 1771, was the fourth in the mission chain; it still stands today about 9 miles (14km) outside L.A. Twenty-six years later, another mission was founded in the nearby San Fernando Valley: Mission San Fernando Rey de España, so named after the King of Spain.

Two other colonial agencies were conceived: the *presidio* (fort) and the *pueblo* (town). Felipe de Neve, the new governor of California, made plans to establish the latter near San Gabriel, at the place the padres had so highly recommended. Despite incentives of land and livestock, it took months to recruit any settlers. Finally in 1781, a bedraggled group of 11 men, 11 women and their 22 children arrived at the mission from Mexico. On 4 September, they proceeded to the chosen spot and ceremoniously founded El Pueblo de Nuestra Señora la Reina de Los Angeles de Porciúncula (Our

*B*ells, not clocks, called the people to work, meals and prayer at Mission San Juan Capistrano.

The 'Apache Spirit' sculpture at the Southwest Museum reflects California's Indian heritage.

Lady the Queen of the Angels of Porciúncula).

Despite its remoteness, by 1800 the population numbered 315 and the pueblo included 30 homes, a town hall, guardhouse, granaries, a church and a central plaza.

The California Ranchos

Meanwhile, de Neve's successor passed new laws enabling him to grant vast tracts of land and grazing rights to settlers. Tens of thousands of acres were distributed in this way, largely to the governor's friends and comrades, and it was not long

before a dozen or so *patrones* (landlords) owned nearly all of what is now coastal Los Angeles County, with the exception of the mission lands and the farms surrounding the pueblo.

Colonial powers customarily controlled all trade between their own territories. Mexico and Spain therefore received the wealth of goods produced by the California ranchos and missions. Returning from the Orient in 1808, a Boston sea captain enthusiastically reported that huge vats of tallow and thousands of hides and sea otter pelts, which would bring high profits in New England, could be had in California for a song. With few Spanish ships or militia in the area to enforce the trading laws, Yankee ships defiantly began to capitalize on this lucrative market, ending California's isolation from the rest of the world.

Mexican Rule

Californian revenues declined substantially during the long Mexican War of Independence, which began in 1810 and lasted for more than a decade. On 26 March 1825, the flag of Spain was taken down and the flag of Mexico raised above the pueblo's plaza; this was the only sign giving any indication that the former Spanish territory was now part of the Republic of Mexico.

At the time that the missions were established, it was believed that after about 10 years of guidance under the padres, the Indians would be ready to become 'citizens' and receive their own allotments of land. However, the patriarchal system did not foster the Indians' sense of self-reliance and the missions continued to hold the land in trust until the native population was deemed capable of supporting itself.

In 1835, the Mexican government introduced a plan of secularization. The padres were ordered out of California and commissioners were appoint-ed to distribute 8 million acres (3 million ha) of mission land and resources. Most of the Indians were soon swindled out of their shares by unscrupulous ranchers and either fled to the mountains or found themselves having to work for the dons in order to survive. Thus, almost overnight, the missions which had once been the pride of Spanish America were destroyed, and with them went the irreplaceable culture of the indigenous people.

Meanwhile, the pueblo of Los Angeles had become the largest settlement in the territory with a population of nearly 1,250. During the twenty five years of Mexican rule, a number of Americans – some by chance and some by choice – had reached California. They joined the Catholic church and married into the leading families of the area, and within a few years had become great landholders, wielding a monopoly on local commerce.

When war erupted between the United States and Mexico in 1846, agitators in Washington were already calling for **15** the annexation of California. In fact, the dispute was really over the annexation of Texas the previous year, but the conflict soon spread and engulfed all Mexican territories north of the Rio Grande. The Californians put up a good fight, often resisting forces several times their number, as they did at the bloody battle of San Pasqual. Eventually however, they were outnumbered, and in January 1847 General Andrés Pico had to relinquish Los Angeles to the Americans.

After the Gold Rush

Los Angeles's fortunes did not start to change, however, until gold was discovered in northern California in 1848. The result was that many Angelenos packed their bags and headed straight for the gold fields, but those who stayed behind found a lucrative market in supplying food and goods to the miners. Meat replaced hides and tallow as the main industry of the ranches and cattle were herded north where they could be sold for 10 times the going rate.

On 4 April 1850, the city of Los Angeles was incorporated and declared the county seat. Its first newspaper, *The Star*, was printed the same year in both Spanish and English.

Over the next 20 years, Los Angeles became renowned as a 'bad' town, with the largest number per capita of gambling dens, brothels and saloons in the West. Simultaneously, new industries were springing up: local vineyards flourished and wine became an important export; the area's first citrus trees were planted; and in 1863, a water-supply system that used wooden pipes was installed.

During the Civil War, California pledged allegiance to the Union, although there were many Southern sympathizers. Of greater concern to the Angelenos was the drought of 1862-64, in which thousands of cattle perished from thirst and starvation. It was decades before the region's most profitable industry recovered.

Los Angeles began to lose its wild, frontier-town character after the war. The first railway was constructed in 1869 –

to the harbour at San Pedro – and shipments of wine, fruit, wheat and other agricultural products replaced cattle as a main source of income. At this time, many Chinese labourers who had emigrated to work the transcontinental railroad settled in L.A. One of the city's worst incidents of racial violence occurred in 1871, when the murder of a white policeman unleashed an angry mob who raged through Chinatown and hanged 19 Orientals.

The Boom Years

By 1870, Los Angeles's population numbered 5,614. Hotels and larger buildings went up, and civic cultural institutions such as a library, dance academy and drama society were inaugurated. Further prosperity followed in 1876, with the extension of the Southern Pacific Railroad to Los Angeles making the vital transcontinental link and setting the stage for the most phenomenal real estate boom the nation had seen.

For some time previously, Southern California had been

Spirits of the West: the Gene Autry Western Heritage Museum glorifies the life of the cowboy.

attracting a steady trickle of settlers from the East, lured by the mild climate and beautiful landscape. As the large ranchos were divided, the settlers planted orchards and gardens **17** and introduced modern agricultural methods. Oranges became one of the major crops, and the invention of the refrigerated rail car meant that they could be shipped nationwide, fuelling the region's reputation as a Garden of Eden.

In late 1885, the Santa Fe Railroad reached Los Angeles and the two competitor lines started a fierce rate war. With all the frenzy of a gold rush, people set out for a new life in the promised land. Soon professional speculators arrived and property prices skyrocketed. After the Los Angeles city lots had been sold, new communities were staked out and by the end of 1887 there were 25 satellite towns dotted along the railroad. One of these, created by Horace and Daeida Wilcox when they sub-divided their 120-acre (48ha) orchard, was called Hollywood.

The boom collapsed about 2½ years after it had begun, but by the time the dust had settled in 1890, Los Angeles had embarked on a new campaign, designed to bring not speculators but the hardworking farmers of

V*anity boards tower above Sunset Strip, set against the backdrop of the Hollywood Hills.*

the Midwest. California's prize agricultural produce was vigorously promoted and people started pouring in.

The discovery of petroleum not far from the city centre in 1892 prompted another flurry of development. The first well, drilled by Edward Doheny and Charles Canfield, yielded 45 barrels a day. Within five years nearly 2,500 wells had been sunk within the city limits, and the industry flourished. Led by Los Angeles, California went on to produce a quarter of the world's oil supply right into the 20th century.

One of the most significant events of the 1890s was the construction of a deep-water harbour. A long battle over the site had been waged between the Southern Pacific Railroad – which favoured development near its terminal in Santa Monica – and the public, who were

demanding a free port. After three congressional hearings, San Pedro was approved as the harbour site, and in 1910 the Port of Los Angeles was officially opened, the largest man-made port in the world.

The 20th Century

At the beginning of the 20th century, Los Angeles was a dynamic city with a population of over 100,000 people. A new advertising venture, with the slogan 'Oranges for Health – California for Wealth', and an expanded campaign in the following years, caused the population of the city to triple over the next decade.

Only one thing stood in the way of expansion: water, or rather, the lack of it. As the population mushroomed, it became clear that the Los Angeles River, the sole source of water for the city, would not be able to support its needs.

William Mulholland, at that time chief engineer of the Municipal Water Bureau, devised a scheme to obtain water from the Owens River valley, which was fed by snow melt from the High Sierras. In one of California's amazing feats of determination, an aqueduct with **19** a total length of over 233 miles (375km) was constructed, designed to deliver enough water for a city of 2 million. As an added benefit, a hydroelectric generating plant was completed along the aqueduct in 1917, paving the way for increased industrial expansion.

In 1923, with the population rising by 100,000 each year, it was clear that an additional supply of water would soon be needed. Mulholland began to survey a route for a waterway from the Colorado River, 400 miles (644km) away in Arizona. The waterway was constructed and the new system delivered its first drop to Los Angeles in 1939.

After World War I, the Los Angeles of the 1920s became the fastest growing city in the United States. With 12 annexations in 1923 alone, the metropolis of Los Angeles soon stretched all the way from the southern harbour to the San Fernando Valley. Citrus crops accounted for one third of the county's produce sales. It was the country's richest, as well as its most diversified, agricultural region. Large oil refineries went up, and with the coming of Firestone and Goodyear, it also became a major rubber producing centre. Later, both aircraft and automobile assembly plants were built. No industry, however, was – or is – as enduring in Los Angeles as that of motion pictures, which in 1919 was already producing 80 percent of the world's supply. It has remained the city's chief industry to this day.

Personal wealth was high, and the Great Depression in 1929 hit hard. Yet, Southern California proved a magnet for the dispossessed farmers of the Dust Bowl region (south central USA), and a long line of migrants headed west, further boosting the population. By 1935, the city was recovering economically and ranked fifth among the industrial counties of the US.

World War II brought further industrial and population growth as workers flocked to L.A. to find jobs in the aircraft plants and shipyards. By 1963, California had become America's most populous state.

*C*ity Hall, once L.A.'s tallest building, shines through the Music Center's synchronized fountain.

There was a limit, however, to how much growth even this land of plenty could cope with. With the postwar population boom came more water shortages, reduced services and increased racial tension. In the summer of 1965, widespread rioting broke out in the black ghetto of Watts, in south central Los Angeles. Six days of vandalism, looting and fires left 34 people dead and caused $40 million worth of damage.

This grizzly scene was repeated in the spring of 1992, with the acquittal of four white policemen accused of beating black motorist Rodney King, sparking 48 hours of violence. The death toll reached 50, plus thousands injured and property damage of over $1 billion. It was America's most destructive civil unrest this century.

As Los Angeles County approaches the year 2000, when its population is likely to top 10 million, it is challenged by a myriad of social problems, from homelessness to lack of water. Having to contend with events such as the 1994 earthquake only exacerbates the situation. However, despite the declining social services and overstrained infrastructure, it is still a place of hope to thousands of people worldwide: for so many, it will always be a symbol of the dream of health and prosperity, which it generated itself so many years ago. **21**

What to See

Look at L.A. as one big movie studio backlot. Here you can go from set to set, from beach to boulevard, with as many complete scene changes as you like in one day.

When setting out for your destination, don't automatically take to the freeway, especially if you don't have far to go – average commuter speed during rush hours is now down to 20mph (30kph), and you can often make better time on the streets. Distance in L.A. is measured in time, not miles!

Downtown Los Angeles

People used to joke that Los Angeles didn't have a downtown. What they meant was that the region defined by three freeways and the river doesn't fit the mould of the equivalent areas of other cities of its size and stature. Nightlife here is quiet and hidden. People don't come here to shop. The town's biggest industry is found elsewhere. Downtown might not be regarded as the heart of the city, but nowhere else claims that distinction in L.A.

In actual fact, downtown is one of L.A.'s most interesting areas, with a core of beautiful historic buildings, bright modern plazas, good restaurants and colourful ethnic enclaves. Several excellent performing arts venues and the centres of politics and finance are located here. In recent years, one of the most ambitious urban renewal projects in the country has given downtown such an exciting facelift that Angelenos who haven't been here in a while are amazed at the result.

Downtown is surprisingly walkable – at least during the day. At dusk, when thousands of commuters pour out of the city and back to the suburbs, the street people become more visible, accosting locals with outstretched paper cups. They are usually more disturbing than dangerous, but it's best to avoid the experience altogether and take a cab. The city can also be explored on the DASH

LOS ANGELES HIGHLIGHTS

For Leading Museums and Gallerys, see p.41. All prices here and throughout the book are correct at press time but subject to change.

Mann's Chinese Theatre and the Walk of Fame, *6925 Hollywood Boulevard, Hollywood;* tel. *(213) 464-8111.* The exterior courtyard is always open; the Walk of Fame is along the street. You'll have to buy a cinema ticket to see Mann's ornate interior, but not to follow the stars! (See p.32)

Cabrillo Marine Aquarium, *3720 Stephen White Drive, San Pedro;* tel. *(310) 548-7562.* Some 40 glass tanks reflect southern California's rich marine life. Tues-Fri noon-5pm, Sat-Sun 10am-5pm. Free; parking $6.60 per car. (See p.65)

Disneyland, *1313 Harbor Boulevard, Anaheim (Orange County);* tel. *(714) 999-4565 or (213) 626-8605 ext 4565.* The original Disney theme park is a hit with children and parents alike. Open daily Sept-May, usually Mon-Fri 10am-6pm, Sat-Sun 9am-midnight, special hours in holidays; summer: extended hours begin Memorial Day (May) until the first week in Sept. Adults: 1-day $30, 2-day $55, 3-day $75; children (3-11): 1-day $24, 2-day $44, 3-day $60. Annual and seasonal passports available. (See p.83)

Knott's Berry Farm, *8039 Beach Boulevard, Buena Park (Orange County);* tel. *(714) 220-5200 (taped info) or (714) 827-1776.* Originally built on a reputation for chicken dinners and boysenberry pies; it has since become a bustling 'Wild West' theme park. Summer: Sun-Thurs 9am-11pm, Fri-Sat 9am-midnight. Winter: Mon-Fri 10am-6pm, Sat 10am-10pm, Sun 10am-7pm; closed for Christmas Day. Holidays: adults $25.95, children (3-11) $15.95, seniors $17.95. All tickets $12.95 after 6pm. (See p.84)

Mission San Juan Capistrano, *Camino Capistrano and Ortega Highway. Visitor Center: 31882 Camino Capistrano, no. 107, San Juan Capistrano (Orange County);* tel. *(714) 248-2048.* Beautiful grounds and interesting adobe buildings stand as a proud reminder of California's Mission days. Open daily 8.30am-5pm. Adults $3, children $2. (See p.89)

Universal Studios Hollywood, *100 Universal Plaza, Universal City;* tel. *(818) 508-9600.* Behind-the-scenes tours and exciting rides make this a top attraction. Summer: open daily at 7.30am; winter: open daily at 9am. Adults $29, children $23. (See p.50) **23**

buses which run through the downtown area during the day, for just 25 cents a ride.

One of the best ways to appreciate the area is to take one of the excellent walking tours given on Saturdays by the Los Angeles Conservancy. Highly recommended is the Pershing Square tour of downtown landmarks; as well as providing you with a wealth of historical information, it includes access to the stunning interiors of edifices like the Guarantee Trust and Edison buildings – where it's all marble pillars and flooring, Hugo Ballin murals and Art Deco styling. A variety of special interest tours are also offered. For information telephone (213) 623-2489 weekdays between 9am and 5pm.

STARTING OUT

The **Los Angeles Visitor and Convention Bureau**, lying on Figueroa Street between 7th Street and Wilshire Boulevard, is a mine of information on attractions throughout the city. Two blocks north, at 5th and Figueroa, the five cylindrical towers of glass at the **Westin Bonaventure Hotel** constitute the city's most futuristic skyscraper. You can survey the area from the revolving restaurant and bar on the 35th floor.

To the east on 5th Street is the distinctive pyramid-topped **Central Library**. A devastating fire, caused by arson, destroyed it in 1986, but it was opened in October 1993 after a $221 million reconstruction.

Across from the library is the 73-storey **First Interstate World Center** – the tallest building on the West Coast, designed by IM Pei. Running alongside the building, the majestic **Bunker Hill Steps** lead to California Plaza, forming a symbolic link between the old downtown and the new. At the start of this century, Bunker Hill was an affluent residential neighbourhood of extravagant Victorian mansions, homes to L.A.'s prominent families.

The **Biltmore** (515 South Olive Street), which opened in 1923, is the *grande dame* of all of L.A.'s downtown hotels. The prestigious Academy Awards were originally launched here

Like a futuristic city ... the Bonaventure Hotel, with restaurants, fast food and a shopping gallery.

in the Crystal Room in 1927, and it is said that the award acquired its name after Bette Davis glanced at a sketch of the statuette pencilled on a napkin and remarked, 'It looks like my Uncle Oscar.' The majestic Rendezvous Court at the Olive Street entrance was originally the hotel lobby – climb the Spanish baroque staircase leading up to the galleria, with its coffered ceiling. On the other side of Olive Street, the landscaped **Pershing Square** is the oldest public park in Los Angeles. Its history as a public commons dates back to 1781.

Art Deco is at its best in the nearby **Oviatt Building** (617 South Olive Street). In 1927, merchant James Oviatt was entranced with the new architectural style that he saw while travelling in Paris, and commissioned René Lalique to design all the decorative glass for

his building, which was home to his haberdashery and penthouse suite. The marvellous doors on the present restaurant contain original Lalique glass. The exterior elevators also retain their original hand-carved oak cabs.

From its terminal situated on 3rd and Hill Streets, the **Angel's Flight** inclined railway, whose first service ran in 1901, carried downtowners up and down Bunker Hill for 68 years. Dismantled in 1969 due to redevelopment of the area, Angel's Flight is now being reconstructed and will operate with its original cable cars. Its **25** new terminus is the **Water-court**, a 1½ acre (½ha) urban garden along Olive Street that features outdoor stages for the performing arts and high-tech, synchronized water fountains. Both the Watercourt and the funicular railway make up part of the $1.2 billion **California Plaza** urban renewal scheme.

CULTURE AND POLITICS

The **Museum of Contemporary Art**, known as MOCA (250 South Grand Avenue), presents major contemporary shows and a rotating permanent collection of international works by such artists as Piet Mondrian, Mark Rothko and Franz Kline. The celebrated Japanese architect Arata Isozaki designed the attractive red sandstone building with its pyramid skylights.

The streets around the Civic Center are the heart of Los Angeles culture and politics. City Hall (200 North Spring Street), built in 1928, was the tallest building in the city until the height restrictions were **26** lifted in 1957. You can survey

the city from the observation deck on the 27th floor. Tours are given weekday mornings, by reservation only (tel. 213/485-4423). You can also take a guided tour of the nearby **Los Angeles Times** complex (202 West 1st Street) and explore behind the scenes at a newspaper printing plant (reservations required, tel. 213/237-5000).

The **Music Center** (at 1st Street and Grand Avenue) is the cultural pride of L.A. The complex surrounds a central plaza with a fabulous undulating fountain. It is comprised of the famous Dorothy Chandler Pavilion, for years the site of the Academy Awards as well as the opera and symphony, the circular Mark Taper Forum and the Ahmanson Theatre. A fourth venue, the Disney Concert Hall, is now under construction and will house the Los Angeles Philharmonic.

Whimsical terracotta ornamentation makes the **Million Dollar Theater** (at 310 South Broadway) one of the highlights of the historic Broadway Theater District. This famous vaudeville and movie theatre,

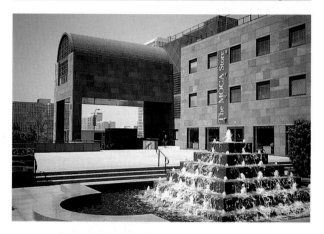

built in 1917, now presents Spanish-language films, as do some of the other ostentatious picture palaces that still stand in the area between 3rd Street and Olympic Boulevard.

Broadway has changed into a bustling Hispanic shopping street, good for bridal gowns, bargain clothing and electronic goods. Don't miss the wonderful murals that pay tribute to the Spanish-speaking clientele of the **Victor Clothing Company** (242 South Broadway). The murals cover both exterior and interior walls, and the in-

The courtyard of the Museum of Contemporary Art constitutes a hallmark of California Plaza.

side is also decorated with the photos of famous patrons who have shopped here since 1920.

Built in 1893, the **Bradbury Building** (at 304 South Broadway) is Los Angeles's oldest commercial building. It is also one of the grandest, with its intricate wrought-iron balconies, marble staircases **27** and open-cage elevators surrounding a skylit atrium court.

Since 1917, **Grand Central Market** (at 317 South Broadway) has adorned the city with a daily cornucopia of enticing fresh produce – fish, poultry, meat and exotic foodstuffs. Today the 40-odd stalls display a wonderful ethnic diversity, where you can sample everything from fresh tortillas to Chinese herbs. It's a great place for browsing and a quick snack or inexpensive lunch.

THE LURE OF THE WEST

The city's first settlement in 1781 was at **El Pueblo de Los Angeles**, now a state historic park at North Main Street and Paseo de la Plaza. The heart of the district is **Olvera Street**, a festive marketplace that sells *piñatas* (papier mâché festive decorations), masks and Mexican handicrafts, with numerous Mexican restaurants and food stalls. The visitors centre (622 North Main Street) provides information on the historical markers of the district, including the Avila Adobe (the

*S*pend some time hunting for festive Mexican handicrafts at the market at Olvera Street.

first house in Los Angeles), the Old Plaza Church, and the shady plaza with its wrought-iron gazebo. Mariachi bands and folk dance groups can usually be seen here at weekends.

In a country that long ago eschewed train travel, the romance of the railway still permeates **Union Station** (800 North Alameda Street). Built in 1939, the handsome Spanish Mission style building has a massive waiting room with arched corridors and a 52ft (16m) high ceiling. In its heyday the station served nearly one million passengers a day; now, it is the hub of L.A.'s new Metro Rail system.

Chinatown lies along North Broadway between Spring and Hill Streets. Here, restaurants, souvenir shops, dim sum parlours and Chinese groceries fan out from the central pedestrian mall, Gin Ling Way, with

its ceremonial gates and exotic Oriental dragons.

The Japanese counterpart, **Little Tokyo**, is situated east of downtown on the streets around 1st and Central. A medieval fire tower marks the entrance to the Japanese Village Plaza shopping mall (327 East 2nd Street). Other community highlights are a cultural centre and theatre, in addition to the Japanese American National Museum (369 East 1st Street).

A third Oriental neighbourhood, **Koreatown**, lies west of downtown along Olympic Boulevard, between Vermont and Western Avenues. All the signs here are in Korean; there are a multitude of restaurants and a large shoping mall of Korean stores at Koreatown Plaza (Western and San Marino). This area was badly damaged during the riots of 1992.

DOWNTOWN MUSEUMS

North of downtown, past the Dodger Stadium, the **Southwest Museum** (234 Museum Drive) perches on a hillside **29** above the Pasadena Freeway (follow signs from the Avenue 43 exit). It is home to a remarkable collection of Native American art and artifacts. The exhibits on tribal life are highly informative and include a number of excellent examples of musical instruments, kachina dolls, and pipes, and a large basketry display. Other historical sights can be found in nearby Highland Park (see p.31).

South of the central downtown area, **Exposition Park** at

The lions, tigers and bears at the Natural History Museum's Discovery Center don't bite.

Vermont and Crenshaw is the site of several museums and attractions, including the Los Angeles Memorial Coliseum and Sports Arena and the 14 acre (6ha) Rose Garden.

The **Natural History Museum of Los Angeles County** (900 Exposition Boulevard) is popular for its dinosaur skeletons and prehistoric fossils. Among the highlights of some three dozen galleries are dioramas of animals in their natural habitats, an impressive mounted megamouth shark, a collection of pre-Columbian artifacts, major exhibits on American history, and the Hall of Birds, with its animated rainforest. The excellent Discovery Center is a hands-on museum for children (see p.109).

The **California Museum of Science and Industry** (at 700 State Drive) presents exhibits from robotics and fibre optics to a miniature winery. At the Aerospace Complex there are rockets, satellites and an impressive **IMAX theatre**.

Rotating exhibitions on the African-American experience in the USA are offered at Ex-

Los Angeles Architecture

The Mission Revival style of architecture abounds in Southern California. It resembles the adobe buildings of the Spanish colonial period, with a central courtyard, arched windows and a square tower. Examples include Union Station, the Southwest Museum, and the Bowers Museum in Orange County.

Several unique buildings lie in Highland Park. **Casa de Adobe** (4605 Figueroa Street) is a re-creation of a 19th-century hacienda from the rancho era, while **El Alisal** (200 East Avenue 43) was home to Charles Fletcher Lummis, founder of the Southwest Museum (see p.29).

Over the freeway, **Heritage Square** (3800 North Homer Street) is a collection of historic buildings, built between 1845 and 1914 and moved here from around the city.

The **Hollyhock House** (4800 Hollywood Boulevard) is the first of various L.A. houses designed by Frank Lloyd Wright, built in 1921 for the heiress Alice Barnsdall.

The **Gamble House** in Pasadena (see p.54) was built by Charles and Henry Greene and is a fine example of the Craftsman-style bungalows that flourished in the early 20th century.

Among the many Art Deco masterpieces are buildings such as the former **I Magnin Bullocks Wilshire** (3050 Wilshire Boulevard) department store and the **Wiltern Theater** at Western and Wilshire, covered in turquoise, terracotta tiles.

L.A.'s hottest contemporary architect is Frank Gehry. His works include the **Edgemar Complex** on Santa Monica's Main Street and San Pedro's **Cabrillo Marine Aquarium**.

position Park, where the **California Afro-American Museum** has become a showcase for black history and culture.

Also nearby is the **Skirball Museum** (3077 University Avenue), with a range of exhibits on Judaism. The **University of Southern California (USC)**, which is renowned for its athletic achievements, lies adjacent to Exposition Park.

31

Hollywood

L.A.'s most lasting landmark is the **Hollywood sign** that sits on top of Beachwood Canyon. Erected in 1923 to promote a new property development, the 50ft (15m) high letters originally spelled out 'Hollywoodland' and were emblazened at night by thousands of lightbulbs (tended by a caretaker who lived in a cabin behind one of the L's). Good views of the sign can be enjoyed from Griffith Park and along Mullholland Drive.

Hollywood became the centre of the film industry in the 1920s, after Cecil B DeMille set up the town's first movie studio near Sunset and Vine in a horse barn and filmed *The Squaw Man*, the first feature-length film, in 1913. The structure now stands on Highland Avenue across from the Hollywood Bowl, where it has been preserved as the **Hollywood Studio Museum**, devoted to artifacts rescued from the studios of the silent film era.

For more than three decades, Hollywood was the epitome of glamour, home to such famous names as Marilyn Monroe and Judy Garland. It is hard to believe that this centre of style could decline into the seedy haunt of hustlers, whores and lost souls who wander Hollywood Boulevard today.

Like a faded movie queen, however, Hollywood lives on its legends. It still holds court among thousands of tourists who flock here by the busload to pay tribute at Mann's Chinese Theatre and follow the Walk of Fame. A long-term revitalization project, launched in 1991, is aimed at restoring the area and its landmarks.

TINSELTOWN TRIUMPHS

The exotic pagoda roof and Oriental sculptures that decorate **Mann's Chinese Theatre** (6925 Hollywood Boulevard) are true Hollywood whimsy. It

*S*tar hunting along the length of the Hollywood Walk of Fame is a time-honoured tradition.

was built by the great show-man Sid Graumann in 1927 and for years carried his name. The famous forecourt with the hand- and footprints of the stars began when actress Constance Talmadge accidentally stepped in wet cement at the grand opening. Among the famous signatures are imprints of Jimmy Durante's nose and Betty Grable's legs.

The Chinese theatre is one of many lavish art deco picture palaces which lined Hollywood Boulevard in its heyday.

Famous Last Resting Places

A few blocks from Paramount is the **Hollywood Memorial Cemetery**, where many stars are buried. The graves of Cecil B DeMille and Douglas Fairbanks Sr can be found in the lake area. The Cathedral Mausoleum holds Rudolph Valentino's crypt, which was visited by the mysterious Lady in Black each year on the anniversary of his death, until she died in 1989.

Westwood Memorial Cemetery boasts one of the most famous graves in all Los Angeles, that of Marilyn Monroe. Her former husband, Joe DiMaggio, adorned her simple wall crypt with roses every week for 25 years after her death. Natalie Wood and Richard Conte are also buried here.

Two branches of **Forest Lawn Memorial Park** offer a pleasant retreat from the city. The Glendale branch is full of marble statuary and mammoth artworks, including a stained-glass replica of Leonardo da Vinci's *The Last Supper* and *The Crucifixion* by Jan Styka. Errol Flynn, Walt Disney, Humphrey Bogart and Spencer Tracy are just a few of the many stars who are buried here. The crypts of Nat King Cole, Clara Bow and Alan Ladd can be found in the Freedom Mausoleum, while those of Clark Gable, Carole Lombard and Jean Harlow are located in the Great Mausoleum.

Monuments to American patriotism adorn the grounds of the sister branch in the Hollywood Hills, where Buster Keaton, Stan Laurel, Charles Laughton and Liberace are buried.

Several of them still stand in an eight-block area known as the Cinema District. *Citizen Kane* premièred at the **El Capitan Theatre** (6838 Hollywood Boulevard) in 1941. It is now the première venue for Disney films. **The Egyptian** (6712 Hollywood Boulevard), was Hollywood's first movie palace, and has also been renovated. Graumann built this one in 1922, after the discovery of King Tutankhamen's tomb.

As you meander in and out of the Tinseltown landmarks, you are literally following the stars. Nearly 2,000 bronze and terrazzo stars honouring celebrities in the fields of music and entertainment are embedded in the pavement. This is the **Hollywood Walk of Fame**, and it stretches for 3½ miles (5½km) along Hollywood Boulevard, right from Sycamore Avenue to Gower Street, and along Vine Street from Yucca Street to Sunset Boulevard. Among the most sought-after stars are those of Marilyn Monroe (in front of McDonald's at 6774 Hollywood Boulevard), Charlie Chaplin (at 6751) and John

*T*he art deco picture palace, El Capitan is a movie buff's 'must' and a landmark in its own right.

Wayne (1541 Vine). An additional 500 blank stars are waiting to honour the stars of the future. To attain such concrete notoriety, you must be nominated to the Hollywood Chamber of Commerce, and then, if selected, come up with a total of $3,500 for your star. **35**

Opened in 1927, the Hollywood Roosevelt Hotel (7000 Hollywood Boulevard) fast established itself as *the* hotel of the film world, notably hosting the first public Oscar ceremony two years later. The lobby features hand-painted ceilings and Spanish revival décor of wrought-iron grill work. On display on the mezzanine floor are historic Hollywood photographs and memorabilia.

Judy Garland once worked as a waitress across the street at **CC Brown's** (7007 Hollywood Boulevard). This atmospheric, 1920s malt shop was also where the hot fudge sundae was invented.

HOLLYWOOD MANIA

A *Tyrannosaurus rex* known as Bruce towers above **Ripley's Believe It or Not!** at the corner of Hollywood Boulevard and Highland. Robert Ripley was a cartoonist who travelled the far corners of the globe in the 1930s and '40s, searching for the bizarre. His first 'Odditorium' opened at the Chicago World's Fair in 1933 and the cartoon features based on his collection are still syndicated worldwide. Found among the (grotesque) curiosities on display here are a real shrunken head, a two-headed goat and a man-eating clam.

Around the corner on Highland is the **Max Factor Museum of Beauty**, where you can see celebrity hairpieces and make-up rooms, and hundreds of star photographs in a tribute to the man who made make-up an art form in itself.

Next door to Ripley's is the **Guinness World of Records**, offering two floors of amazing facts, feats and achievements. Across the street, the **Hollywood Wax Museum** can also be visited on a joint ticket. The museum features an eclectic collection of superstars, from Jesus Christ to Sylvester Stallone, as well as a gruesome Chamber of Horrors.

Further along, **Frederick's of Hollywood**, which is well known and loved for its trashy lingerie, houses a Bra Museum where you can peek at star-studded undergarments – from Marilyn's to Madonna's.

Hollywood and Vine was once touted as the heart of Tinseltown, but is now a nondescript intersection. Nearby is the unusual **Capitol Records Building**, which is shaped like a stack of records. Its distinctive design is accredited to recording stars Nat King Cole and Johnny Mercer.

Paramount Studios (5555 Melrose Avenue) is the only motion picture studio which is still physically located in Hollywood. You can see the backlot on a walking tour that takes you through the studios, film sets (when not in use), sound stage and props department, and which gives a glimpse of other behind-the-scenes activities. The tour reveals various tricks of the trade, like the B-tank, where Moses parted the waters for the *Ten Commandments*, and New York Street, a façade of brownstones made of fiberglass and aged to look like real brick.

Paramount Studios is edged by **Melrose Avenue** on the south, a retail stretch of unique shops that runs into the separate city of West Hollywood.

*F*ew visitors can resist a peek at America's most famous lingerie shop, Frederick's of Hollywood.

The blocks between La Brea and Fairfax are referred to as 'trendy Melrose', where L.A.'s hippest youngsters sport wild hairdos and outlandish fashions. Spiced with wacky designs and bright colours, the indvidual storefronts proffer one-off boutiques, chic restaurants, and cafés and diners. **37**

The Wilshire District

Wilshire Boulevard began as an Indian trail connecting the downtown area with the La Brea tar pits. Today it is one of the widest and longest boulevards in North America, and showcases the changing faces of Los Angeles. Stretching 16 miles (25km) from downtown to the sea, it passes through a variety of ethnic neighbourhoods, as well as all financial brackets – from the very poor to the ridiculously wealthy. The mid-Wilshire district just south of Hollywood contains a number of attractions.

In the 1930s, the stretch of Wilshire between La Brea and Fairfax Avenues was christened the **Miracle Mile** by developers, eager to attract patrons to their classy new shopping district. In spite of the decline of the area in the 1950s and '60s, its Art Deco buildings are now being restored, thanks to increased appreciation in L.A. of the city's architectural heritage. Callender's

Restaurant (5773 Wilshire at Curson Avenue) displays old photographs and a large mural glorifying life on the 'Miracle Mile' during its heyday.

HISTORY IN THE MAKING

The area's main attractions are centred in Hancock Park. Dotted throughout the grounds are the **La Brea Tar Pits**, one of the world's richest sources of Pleistocene fossils, which date back 40,000 years. In the large pit in front of the museum, life-size replicas of mastodons are shown trapped in the tar. From viewing stations alongside other pits, you can watch the on-going excavations and view the amalgamated bones of the unfortunate prehistoric beasts that perished here.

The **George C Page Museum of La Brea Discoveries** (at 5801 Wilshire Boulevard) provides a fascinating insight into Ice Age life in southern California. The 15-minute La Brea Story is a good introductory film that depicts how the animals became trapped in the

HOLLYWOOD/THE WILSHIRE DISTRICT

N

Mulholland Drive

Hollywood Reservoir

Griffith Park

101

Runyon Canyon Park

Hollywood Bowl

Hollywood Studio Museum

Mann's Chinese Theatre

Franklin Avenue

Franklin Avenue

Yucca St

Hollywood W. all of Fame

Hollywood Boulevard

Hollywood Boulevard

Hollywood Roosevelt Hotel

Max Factor Museum

Ripley's Believe It or Not!

Sunset Boulevard

Sunset Boulevard

Fountain Avenue

Fountain Ave

2

Fairfax Avenue

Gardner Street

La Brea Avenue

Orange Drive

Highland Avenue

Sycamore Avenue

HOLLYWOOD

Vine Street

Cahuenga

Gower Street

Van Ness Avenue

Western Avenue

Normandie Avenue

101

Santa Monica Boulevard

2

Downtown LA

Willoughby Avenue

Hollywood Memorial Cemetery

West Hollywood

Melrose Avenue

Paramount Studios

Melrose Avenue

Melrose Avenue

Las Palmas Avenue

Beverly Boulevard

Beverly Boulevard

CBS TV City

Pan Pacific Park

The Wilshire Country Club

Rossmore Avenue

Larchmont

Van Ness Avenue

Farmers Market

3rd Street

3rd Street

3rd Street

LA County Museum of Art

George C. Page Museum

HANCOCK PARK

Hancock Park

La Brea Tar Pits

Wilshire Boulevard

Wilshire Boulevard

Petersen Automotive Museum

San Vicente Boulevard

Olympic Boulevard

Crenshaw Boulevard

Western Avenue

Olympic Boulevard

0 ────── 1 mile

0 ────── 1.5 km

Pico Boulevard

Venice Boulevard

asphalt as they edged down to a pool of water to drink. Skeletons of extinct creatures such as the sabre-tooth cat, imperial mammoth and giant ground sloth have been reconstructed from the fossils. The Warhol-like wall display of 400 dire wolf skulls brings a startling realization of just how many animals have been unearthed here. Scientists have recovered four million fossils to date, but out of the 420 animal species found, only one fossil has been human: the 9,000-year-old 'La Brea Woman'. Killed by a blow to the head, she may have been L.A.'s first murder victim. The museum also features a fishbowl laboratory, where visitors can see fossils being cleaned and catalogued. The peaceful atrium nurtures primitive plants, several of which have evolved over a period of 100 million years.

T rapped in tar: the Ice Age is brought to life at the La Brea Tar Pits in Hancock Park.

ART IN THE MAKING

The **Los Angeles County Museum of Art**, the city's largest, is located next door. Among the many treasures housed in this five-building complex are an important collection of pre-Columbian artifacts originally from Mexico and Peru, American colonial art and furniture, the famous Gilbert monumental silver collection, Japanese masterpieces, and what is generally regarded as the finest Indian and Southeast Asian art

LEADING MUSEUMS AND GALLERIES

Huntington Library, Museum and Botanical Gardens, *1151 Oxford Road, San Marino (Pasadena); tel. (818) 405-2100.* Rare books and manuscripts, British and French 18th- and 19th-century art, and botanical gardens. Tues-Fri 1-4.30pm, and Sat-Sun 10.30am-4.30pm; adults $5; students and children $3. (See p.54)

J Paul Getty Museum, *17985 Pacific Coast Highway, Malibu; tel. (310) 458-2003 for parking reservations.* Greek and Roman antiquities, pre-20th-century Western European painting and illuminated manuscripts. Tues-Sun 10am-5pm. Free. (See p.57)

Los Angeles County Museum of Art, *5905 Wilshire Boulevard, Los Angeles; tel. (213) 857-6010 for current exhibition and gallery rotation information.* Features American art and furniture, pre-Columbian artifacts, Gilbert silver collection, Japanese, Indian and Southeast Asian art. Wed-Thurs 10am-5pm, Fri 10am-9pm, Sat-Sun 11am-5pm; closed Mon, Tues; adults $6; seniors/students $4; children $1. Free 2nd Tuesday of each month. (See p.40)

Natural History Museum of Los Angeles County, *Exposition Park, 900 Exposition Boulevard, Los Angeles; tel. (213) 744-3414, fax: (213) 746-2249.* Dinosaur skeletons, animal dioramas, gems and minerals, birds, American history, and pre-Columbian artifacts. Tues-Sun 10am-5pm; adults $5; seniors/students $2.50; children $1. Free first Tuesday of each month. (See p.30)

Norton Simon Museum, *411 West Colorado Boulevard, Pasadena; tel. (818) 449-3730, fax: (818) 796-4978.* European art from the Renaissance to the mid-20th century. Thurs-Sun noon-6pm; adults $4; seniors/students $2; children free. (See p.55)

Southwest Museum, *234 Museum Drive, Los Angeles; tel. (213) 221-2164.* A remarkable collection of Native American art and artifacts, focusing on the tribes of the Southwest, California, the Great Plains and the Northwest Coast. Follow the signs from Avenue 43 exit of the Pasadena Freeway, 110. Tues-Sun 11am-5pm; adults $5; seniors/students $3; children $2. (See p.29)

Armand Hammer Museum of Art and Cultural Center, *10899 Wilshire Boulevard, Los Angeles; tel. (310) 443-7000.* Collections include five centuries of Western European art, as well as a number of special exhibitions. Tues-Sun 10am-6pm; adults $4.50; seniors/students $3; children 17 and under free. (See p.48)

collection in the West. Unfortunately, cutbacks in funding have forced the museum to adopt a rotating gallery schedule, and many sections are only open during the morning or afternoon. If you are interested in seeing particular collections, then call ahead to determine when you will be

A sculpture garden at the County Museum of Art leads to the Japanese Pavilion.

able to do so. All galleries are open at the weekends and on Friday evenings.

The popular **Craft and Folk Art Museum** has recently reopened in a new facility at 5800 Wilshire Boulevard. On that same stretch, at Fairfax, the new **Petersen Automotive Museum** showcases over 160 distinctive cars and motorcycles, with special exhibits on automotive themes.

LOCAL COLOUR

A few blocks north on Fairfax is the lively **Farmers Market** (6333 West Third Street). In the 1930s a few farmers gathered here in what was then a field at the edge of town to offset the Depression by selling their produce direct to the people. It's been a popular site ever since, and the tidy fruit and vegetable stands are now joined by a maze of shops selling foodstuffs and gifts, and inexpensive food stalls serving a variety of cuisines. You may even spot a celebrity or two, as the market is next door to CBS television studios.

The Westside

Several communities make up the area known as the Westside. They are linked not only by geographical location, but also by image: upmarket and fashionable, with affluent residential neighbourhoods and a selection of L.A.'s finest dining and shopping areas.

While Hollywood is seen as a revered relic, **West Hollywood** – a separate, incorporated city – is on the cutting edge of modern design. Within its tiny 2 sq miles (5 sq km) you will find over 100 restaurants, L.A.'s best known nightclubs, unique shops and the high-powered offices of the entertainment and music industries.

Melrose Avenue and Beverly and Robertson Boulevards are known as the Avenues of Design. The streets here are lined with design showrooms and a growing number of art galleries, including the notable **Pacific Design Center** (8687 Melrose Avenue). You might easily get swallowed up in the 'Blue Whale', as this gigantic, blue-glass building, designed by Cesar Pelli in 1975, is often called. Some 200 showrooms are housed here and in the adjoining Green Center, which displays an impressive range of traditional and contemporary home and office furniture created by famous designers. The showrooms are for trade-only, meaning the only way you can make purchases is if you buy through an interior designer. Visitors are welcome to browse weekdays from 9am to 5pm, and one-hour tours are given daily at 10am.

Spanning the length of West Hollywood is **Santa Monica Boulevard** – the centre of gay and lesbian nightlife. Every year in June, the city holds the Christopher Street West Gay & Lesbian Pride Celebration, a lively two-day festival and parade which has grown into the third largest in California.

SUNSET STRIP

West Hollywood's most famous thoroughfare is the **Sunset Strip**, stretching from the 8200 block of Sunset Boulevard west to Doheny Drive. It **43**

has been an after-hours mecca for music and film stars since the 1920s. Many top comedians started here in clubs such as The Comedy Store, while rock'n'roll legends were born in the dance halls of The Roxy and Whisky A Go Go.

Cruising the hilly, winding street, you can't fail to notice the vanity boards – huge billboards beaming with the faces of celebrities promoting their latest movie or record (or simply themselves). Among the landmarks that you'll pass are **Spago**, the famous restaurant where Wolfgang Puck invented Californian cuisine, and the **St James's Club and Hotel**, a stately art deco masterpiece built in 1931. Called the Sunset Tower, it was the first all-electric apartment building in California. Clark Gable, Errol Flynn and Jean Harlow were three of the many stars who once lived here.

Sunset Plaza (at 8589-8720 Sunset Boulevard) has been an élite shopping area since 1934. This cluster of Georgian-style buildings, designed by Charles Selkirk, was once home to the legendary Mocambo and Trocadero nightclubs. Today the plaza is lined with upmarket, one-of-a-kind speciality shops and pleasant, European-style sidewalk cafés.

BEVERLY HILLS

Hip gives way to chic at Doheny Drive, where the Strip ends and Sunset Boulevard enters **Beverly Hills**. Here, luxurious homes and landscaped lawns sit on some of the most expensive real estate in the world – all a far cry from the turn of the century, when the land was practically worthless, covered with failed oil wells and fields of lima beans.

All that changed in 1912, when a group of developers built the **Beverly Hills Hotel** (9641 Sunset Boulevard). The Spanish colonial-style building was soon dubbed the Pink Palace, and fast became popular with the movie set. Its Polo Lounge is now a notorious watering hole for Hollywood's power brokers. Marilyn Monroe and John Kennedy were said to be among the celebri-

ties who met secretly in the private bungalows. The hotel is now owned – appropriately – by the richest man in the world, the Sultan of Brunei.

In 1920, silent screen stars Mary Pickford and Douglas Fairbanks built their opulent estate, Pickfair, just up the hill, and movie stars such as Charlie Chaplin, Gloria Swanson and Rudolph Valentino also flocked in to establish one of the most concentrated celebrity enclaves in the world. (The homes 'in the hill' are regard-

The mansions of Beverly Hills: manicured gardens and shaded lawns complement stately homes.

ed as somewhat more prestigious than those 'in the flats'.)

It's not surprising that the greatest number of business licenses in Beverly Hills are issued to gardeners. Those who are not busy manicuring the residential lawns are often to be found working in the lovely **45**

Beverly Garden Park, which borders Santa Monica Boulevard for 2 miles (3km) from Doheny to Wilshire.

Other beautiful gardens can be seen at **Greystone Mansion** (905 Loma Vista Drive), the former estate of the oilman Edward Doheny. The grounds open daily 10am to 5pm, but the mansion, which is now the property of the city and is frequently used as a film set, is closed to the public.

Above all, Beverly Hills is renowned for its stylish and upmarket shopping. Any tour of Los Angeles is not complete without a visit to **Rodeo Drive** (note the pronunciation: *Ro-DAY-oh*), where top designers showcase their fashions to a glamorous, sophisticated (and rich) clientele (see p.92).

Star Gazing

Numerous companies offer tours of the many celebrity homes in Beverly Hills. Alternatively, vendors on Hollywood and Sunset Boulevards hawk maps to the homes of the stars; you can always go on your own tour. Here are a few favourites:

Marilyn Monroe and Joe DiMaggio ended their rocky marriage in 1954 at 508 NORTH PALM DRIVE. Elizabeth Taylor and husband Mike Todd were living at 1330 SCHUYLER ROAD when he died in a tragic plane crash in 1958. Lana Turner's lover, Johnny Stompanato, also met a sudden death when he was stabbed by the star's daughter at 730 NORTH BEDFORD DRIVE. George Burns still lives in the unassuming house he shared with Gracie Allen, 720 NORTH MAPLE DRIVE.

Famous neighbours lined up along ROXBURY DRIVE: at number 822, Marlene Dietrich was only one block away from Jimmy Stewart at number 918, while Lucille Ball (1000) and Jack Benny (1002) were next-door neighbours.

Look out especially for the 'Witch's House' at 516 WALDEN DRIVE. Straight out of a fairy tale, it was built as a movie set in 1921 and later moved to these premises.

Anchoring the southern end of this glossy thoroughfare is the **Regent Beverly Wilshire Hotel** (9500 Wilshire Boulevard), a landmark since 1928 and a favourite of celebrities and visiting royalty, some of whom have been known to rent entire floors for their stay. Those on a more limited budget can take afternoon tea in the Lobby Lounge.

A half-hour guided tour of the area's landmarks and residential districts can be taken for a mere $1 on the old-fashioned **Beverly Hills Trolley**. It runs Tuesday through Saturday from 10.30am and can be caught in front of the Chanel boutique – on the corner of Rodeo Drive and Dayton Way.

 CENTURY CITY

Built on 180 acres (73ha) of Twentieth Century Fox's enormous backlot, **Century City** is a sleek Westside business centre of high-rise office towers and high-flying corporations. It's at its best along the Avenue of the Stars between the ABC Entertainment Center and the Century Plaza Hotel, where brightly lit fountains splash in front of the Schubert Theater and the twin Century Park Towers.

Opened in 1993, the **Museum of Tolerance** (9786 West Pico Boulevard) is a moving and thought-provoking experience focusing on two themes. Using high-tech exhibits, the Tolerancenter explores the history of racism and prejudice in America. Of particular note are the interactive video stations exploring the 1992 L.A. riots. The second half of the museum is devoted to Beit Hashoah, or the Holocaust. In a timed tour that moves from stage to stage in a darkened hall, visitors travel through the events of the Holocaust, from the Warsaw ghetto to the death camps. The concepts and technology employed in this museum are impressive, and lend weight to the gravity of the issues. Beit Hashoah alone lasts a full hour, and equal time is really needed to appreciate the first section and archival collection and multimedia learning centre on the second floor. **47**

WESTWOOD

The sprawling campus of the **University of California, Los Angeles (U.C.L.A.)** is situated in Westwood and is a pleasant place for a stroll. The campus has the lovely Romanesque-style Royce Hall, dating from 1929, and the Powell Library. The Murphy Sculpture Garden is the site of works by Henry Moore and Gaston Lachaise. The Mathias Botanical Garden in the south-east section of the campus is also popular. Maps and information are available from the kiosks at the main entrances and at the visitors centre; ask for the free 90-minute campus tours during the week (tel. 310/206-8147).

To the south of the campus, **Westwood Village** is a popular place to catch the latest film. At the village's southern tip, at 10899 Wilshire Boulevard, the **Armand Hammer Museum of Art and Cultural Center** presents a small, exquisite collection of artworks gathered over the past 50 years by the man himself. Housed in a handsome grey and white marble building, the galleries have masterpieces by painters from Rembrandt to Van Gogh, with an extensive collection of lithographs by Honoré Daumier and rare technical drawings by Leonardo Da Vinci. Check out what else is on while there, as the museum regularly hosts special exhibitions.

*B*uilt in the 1930s, Moore Hall is typical of the decorative architecture of U.C.L.A. campus.

The Valleys

When Angelenos refer to 'The Valley' they are talking about the San Fernando Valley, a vast residential area northwest of downtown Los Angeles. It is also the home of some major film and television studios including Universal, Warner Brothers and NBC, located in Burbank and Glendale. Actually, there are three valleys: adjoining San Gabriel and Santa Clarita make up L.A.'s suburban sprawl. All three are separated from the Los Angeles basin by the Santa Monica Mountains.

The best place to appreciate this geographical divide is along **Mullholland Drive**, a scenic road that twists and turns through the mountains from Highway 101 to Ventura County. It is especially beautiful at night, when the lights of the city shimmer below.

The country's largest urban park, **Griffith Park**, separates Burbank and Glendale from Hollywood, and covers over 4,000 acres (1,620ha). There are several entrances into the park; the visitors centre, where you can pick up a free map, is located near the eastern entrance off the Golden State Freeway (Highway 5).

On clear days, the **Observatory** on Mount Hollywood offers good views of the city and the Hollywood sign across the canyon. Exhibits in the Hall of Science include the Foucault Pendulum and a Cosmic Ray Cloud Chamber. Evening visitors can look at the heavens through a 12in (30cm) telescope. The Planetarium theatre presents dramatic astronomical shows several times daily. Evening shows are followed by Laserium light concerts.

The **Los Angeles Zoo**, on the northeastern side of the park, harbours more than 400 different species of animals, birds and reptiles, grouped according to their continental region. The zoo is known for its extensive breeding programme for endangered species.

The adjacent **Gene Autry Western Heritage Museum** offers an impressive collection of historical artifacts, furniture and art reflecting America's **49**

Western tradition. Autry was the king of the balladeer cowboys who rode the range in the films of the 1930s, '40s and '50s, and the museum illustrates the way in which the West was romanticized in art, literature, film and advertising. Included are a display of Colt firearms and bronze sculptures by Frederic Remmington.

Travel Town, an outdoor transportation museum featuring steam locomotives, is also located in the park.

SAN FERNANDO VALLEY

The Valley's biggest attraction is **Universal Studios Hollywood**. The behind-the-scenes tour of this vast studio complex is more like an amusement park ride. Visitors board a tram which travels through famous film sets, being threatened along the way by King Kong, attacked by the killer shark from *Jaws*, and surviving a collapsing bridge, a flash

flood and a bone-shaking simulated 8.3 earthquake. You are then free to explore the magic of Hollywood in attractions such as *Backdraft*, a firestorm of special effects; *Miami Vice*, an explosive performance of stunt action; and *Star Trek Adventure*, where audience members play their favourite roles in a Star Trek production. Possibly the most spectacular ride, however, is Universal's *Back to the Future*, which sends you rocketing through avalanches, molten volcanoes and the jaws of a dinosaur, all of which are made terrifyingly real by a surrounding IMAX screen. Although you can expect a long wait for the major attractions, musical street shows are at hand to entertain you.

L.A.'s newest shopping and dining area, **CityWalk**, joins Universal. It is full of unique shops and fun, informal restaurants, and boasts a host of whimsical storefronts which make it an amusement park in itself. At night these are lit up in brilliant neon. For neon fans, there's even a Museum of Neon that's worth a visit.

*U*niversal Citywalk: a splash with the kids (left); Captain Coconuts greets shoppers (above).

Nothing is staged just for guests at the nearby **Warner Bros Studios** (at 4000 Warner Boulevard). Here the two-hour VIP tour alters daily, depending on shooting schedules, as small groups of 12 guests walk through the backlot past familiar TV and movie sets and tour production facilities. If scheduling allows, guests are permitted to watch rehearsals and the filming of TV shows. **51**

One of California's finest missions lies in the northern San Fernando Valley. **Mission San Fernando Rey de España** (Mission Hills – 15151 San Fernando Mission Boulevard) was built in 1797 and named for Ferdinand III, King of Spain. Both the grounds and buildings have been beautifully restored, including the *convento* with its Roman arches and painted Indian motifs, the church with a gold-leafed reredos (ornamental screen) from the 16th-century at the back of the altar, and the workshops.

SAN GABRIEL VALLEY

The lush orange and lemon groves that blossomed in the San Gabriel Valley 100 years ago have all but disappeared, but this prosperous suburban area still has a wealth of botanical delights. The **Los Angeles State and County Arboretum** is to be found here, nurturing plants from every part of the world. Stretching along the lower slopes of the San Gabriel Mountains, **Descanso Gardens** are known for their vast camellia displays and historic collection of roses.

The wealthiest of California's missions was the fourth to be built in the chain (see p.12), **Mission San Gabriel Arcangel** (537 West Mission Drive, San Gabriel). Because of earthquake damage in 1988, the chapel, museum and winery have been closed, but the gardens and cemetery are still open to the public daily.

Nestling beneath the snow-capped San Gabriel Mountains, the city of **Pasadena** has remained true to its Chippewa Indian name, meaning 'Crown of the Valley'. Attracted by its balmy weather and luscious orange groves, midwesterners flocked here in the 1880s, intent on establishing a cultural climate as invigorating as the natural one. Development was fast and, by the turn of the century, wealthy easterners had built grand mansions and hotels for those vacationing during the winter. Pasadena soon became a popular resort area.

This legacy is apparent in the handsome homes that are strung along the wide, shaded

boulevards and in the grand dome of **Pasadena City Hall**, which was built in 1927. The stretch of Colorado Boulevard nearby forms the heart of **Old Town Pasadena**. These eleven blocks are full of historic Victorian buildings that have been restored and the area has been converted into a bustling shopping and dining district.

Pasadena is famous for the **Rose Bowl** stadium where, at full capacity, 103,000 spectators can watch the annual college football championship on New Year's Day. Prior to the

The Victorian buildings around Old Town Pasadena make for a delightful shopping district.

game, one million people line Colorado Boulevard to see the fabulous floats in the **Tournament of Roses Parade**, a tradition for over 100 years. You can view the stadium outside game times ($2), or during the monthly swap meet (see p.94).

An outstanding example of Pasadena's architecture can be **53**

seen in the **Gamble House** (4 Westmoreland Place). Built in 1908 by the architects Greene and Greene, it is an internationally recognized masterpiece of the Arts and Crafts Movement which flourished at the turn of the century. Every detail of the house, from the hand-rubbed fine woods and original furniture to the beautiful Tiffany art glass windows and light fixtures, was custom designed by the architects for David and Mary Gamble, of Proctor and Gamble fame.

The **Fenyes Mansion** (470 West Walnut Street) houses the Pasadena Historical Society, and a Finnish folk art collection. The original furnishings and artworks reveal the cultured life that was enjoyed at the turn of the century along Orange Grove Avenue, then known as 'Millionaires' Row'.

Pasadena is home to two of the best museums in L.A. **The Huntington Library, Museum and Botanical Gardens** is the site of the superb collections of railroad tycoon Henry E Huntington. It's impossible to do justice to everything here in a single afternoon, so try to see your main areas of interest

*W*eird and wonderful – fascinating cacti flourish in the Huntington Desert Garden.

first and also be sure to leave time for a peaceful wander in the beautiful gardens.

The library is one of the most complete research facilities in the world. Among the rare books and manuscripts here are a Gutenberg bible and the original illustrated Ellesmere manuscript of Chaucer's *Canterbury Tales*.

The three art galleries contain one of the most comprehensive collections of British and French 18th- and 19th-century art in the whole of America. Gainsborough's *Blue Boy* and Lawrence's *Pinkie* are the showpieces of the Huntington Gallery. At the Virginia Steele Scott Gallery you can view American paintings from the 1730s to 1930s, while the Arabella Huntington Collection shows Renaissance paintings and 18th-century French decorative arts.

The lovely Botanical Gardens offer 130 acres (50ha) of changing landscapes. Among the highlights are the Desert Garden with a vast maze of mature cacti, the Japanese garden with its drum bridge and the much-praised Rose Garden showing the history of the rose over 2,000 years.

A stunning seven centuries of European art are on show at the **Norton Simon Museum** (at 411 West Colorado Boulevard). It is considered to be one of the world's finest collections, with masterpieces by Rembrandt, Goya, Picasso and the Impressionists. In addition there is an extensive collection of Degas sculptures, as well as works by Rodin. As a perfect complement to the Western art there is an outstanding selection of sculpture from India and Southeast Asia spanning a period of 2,000 years.

The **Pacific Asia Museum** (46 North Los Robles Drive) has been designed to resemble a Chinese Imperial palace. It houses a contemporary Asian arts gallery and also has a real Chinese courtyard garden.

Coastal Los Angeles

From Malibu in the north to Long Beach in the south, the shoreline communities of Los Angeles County stretch for 72 miles (115km) along the edge of the ocean. It's possible, but not practical, to drive the entire length along the coast. For a start, you'll want to circumvent the sorry stretch of road by the airport, and the residential areas between Manhattan and Redondo beaches, which are chock-a-block with houses and stop signs.

For sheer scenic pleasure, however, Pacific Coast Highway 1 (often signposted PCH) leading north from Santa Monica to Malibu and beyond can't be beat. Palos Verdes Drive is another beautiful stretch, hugging the cliffs along the southern tip of Santa Monica Bay.

MALIBU

Malibu is best known for its exclusive beachfront colonies, home to movie stars since the 1930s. You'll only get to see the backsides of these expensive bungalows as you travel the ribbon of highway that lies between the mountains and the sea. Sadly, many homes were destroyed by the brush fires and mudslides of 1993-94; but there are several beach access points where you can still admire the rolling surf and idyllic beach life that has done so much to make Malibu famous.

One such place is **Malibu Pier**, a popular spot for fishing. Constructed in 1905 and rebuilt several times since, this was the main connection with the south until the state highway was built in 1929.

Another is **Malibu Lagoon State Park**, one of the few remaining wetlands in California. Several boardwalks extend into the marsh, where you can see shorebirds such as the Great Blue Heron and American Avocet. A popular surfing beach adjoins the lagoon.

It is also possible to explore this unique coastal environment from the grounds of the **Adamson House**. This Spanish colonial revival home contains magnificent examples of the admired decorative ceramic tiles produced by Malibu Potteries in the late 1920s.

Malibu's cultural plum is the wonderful **J Paul Getty Museum**, which was purpose built to house the millionaire's personal collection (which has since been greatly expanded). The museum is a re-creation of Villa dei Papiri, a Roman villa destroyed by the terrible eruption of Mount Vesuvius in AD 79. Even the splendid gardens are authentic, with trees, flowers and herbs that could have been found 2,000 years ago.

The museum is renowned for its outstanding collection of Greek and Roman antiquities, with some objects dating from as far back as 3000 BC. **57**

The J Paul Getty Museum is an authentic re-creation of a Roman villa, housing precious antiquities.

*T*he grounds of the J Paul Getty Museum are the setting for some handsome statuary.

Amongst its most important works are the Cycladic Harpist from the early Bronze Age and the Greek bronze of the Victorious Athlete from the late 4th century BC. The upper level of the museum holds fine Renaissance and Baroque paintings, drawings by the Old Masters, and a selection of 18th-century **58** French decorative arts.

Although admission to the museum is free, a strict parking policy requires that reservations are made in advance, up to two weeks ahead during busy seasons. No side street parking is available, and walkin visitors are not permitted. Visitors planning to arrive by bus, taxi or motorcycle should also call this number for information: (310) 458-2003.

PCH meets the western terminus of Sunset Boulevard. Follow this winding road into the hills and you will enter the well-to-do residential enclave of Pacific Palisades. A few miles along is the turn-off for **Will Rogers State Historic Park**, a 186-acre (75ha) ranch which belonged to the late cowboy humorist. Tours of the ranch house illustrate some of Rogers' eccentricities: a porch swing in the living room and a raised ceiling that allowed him to practise rope tricks indoors. Rogers was an enthusiastic horseman and polo player, and weekend games are still held on the polo field in the front yard. A system of hiking trails extends into the park.

SANTA MONICA TO MARINA DEL REY

Ever since it was founded in the 1870s, **Santa Monica** has been thought of as the perfect seaside town. Nonetheless, in the 1930s, poker games, bingo parlours and a casino barge anchored offshore brought such notoriety that the author Raymond Chandler used it as a model for the freewheeling Bay City of his detective novels. Today, with trendy boutiques, blue-chip art galleries, a buzzing nightlife scene and some of L.A.'s finest restaurants, Santa Monica looks set to continue forever as L.A.'s most popular playground.

Santa Monica Pier, site of the famous carousel as well as the La Monica Ballroom, was built in 1908. Much of this historic structure was demolished by storms in 1983, prompting an authentic restoration. The

*S*oak up traditional seaside amusements, night or day, along the popular Santa Monica Pier.

arcades lining the pier have a wonderfully tacky ambience, and more development is underway, including a Fun Zone with 12 rides, such as a Ferris wheel and new roller coaster. You can ride the carousel with its hand-crafted wooden horses or rent fishing tackle at the end of the pier. The free summer concerts are popular.

Volleyball and biking are just two ways of keeping fit for (and on) the beach in Santa Monica.

Beneath the pier stretches the widest band of sand on the Pacific Coast. A bicycle path runs alongside the beach to Venice; you can rent bikes and roller blades at nearby hotels. Remember not to walk on the bike path – you could get run over, or even be given a ticket! Use the footpath instead.

Palisades Park is a pretty, palm-lined stretch that runs for one mile (1.5km) along Ocean Avenue. The broad walkway offers spectacular views of the ocean, especially at sunset.

Main Street is awash with unusual shops and excellent restaurants (see pp.92). Looming right over its southern end at the intersection with Rose Avenue, is a giant sculpture by Jonathan Borofsky known as *Ballerina Clown*. This controversial piece – a clown's head on a tutu-clad body – seems to symbolize the air of clever and cultured frivolity that pervades much of the city.

The Edgemar complex in the 2400 block was at one time an egg-processing plant, but has since been rescued and restored by L.A.'s favourite post-

Beaches

Blue skies, white sands and rolling surf – nothing says Southern California like the beach! Observe the rules (see p.118) and enjoy L.A. and Orange County's most popular beaches.

Set against the backdrop of the Santa Monica Mountains, the beaches along Pacific Coast Highway at Malibu are some of the most scenic. At **Malibu Surfrider Beach** you'll find some of the best surfing around. **Santa Monica Beach** and **Venice Beach** are two of the most popular, due to the wealth of activities along the adjoining boardwalk and pleasure pier.

Manhattan, Hermosa and Redondo are referred to as the **South Bay beaches**. California's beach culture started here, when George Freeth first caught the waves at Redondo Beach in 1907 – the Beach Boys immortalized the surfer's life in song in the '60s. These beaches are popular with locals.

True to its name, **Long Beach** boasts an extensive 5½ miles (9km) of beach, with numerous watersports and activities.

Orange County has some of the area's best beaches. **Bolsa Chica State Beach** is a beautiful 6-mile (9½km) stretch that adjoins a wetlands ecological reserve. The gentle surf makes it a good spot for both swimmers and families. Adjacent **Huntington Beach** is one of the world's great surfing spots.

Newport Beach and **Balboa Beach**, joined by a busy bike path, are the most popular spots on this part of the coast.

Main Beach lies smack in the middle of town at Laguna Beach, and the wooden boardwalk rivals few others as a vantage place from where to watch the locals at play.

modern architect, Frank Gehry (a Santa Monica resident). It now houses a restaurant, bookstore and the **Santa Monica Museum of Art**, which showcases the avant garde and performance art of contemporary Southern California artists.

Santa Monica artists also put on shows in the second-floor galleries of the **Heritage Museum** (2612 Main Street). **61**

This former Victorian home was moved to Main Street and its lower floor has been restored to reflect a turn-of-the-century lifestyle. The upstairs rooms are reserved for exhibitions. Dozens of prominent art galleries have set up shop in Santa Monica, with the result that it is now a major centre of L.A.'s contemporary art scene. Many shops are situated in a pocket of Colorado Avenue, between 9th and 10th Streets.

Street Art

Santa Monica and Venice have attracted so many artists that any blank slab of concrete is fair game for an outdoor canvas.

Santa Monica has about two dozen murals, three of which can be seen along Ocean Park Boulevard. At the corner with Main Street, passengers wait for the bus alongside Victorian characters from *Santa Monica at the Turn of the Century*. Further up the street, underneath the 4th Street overpass, various sea creatures from *Save the Whale* frolic on one side, across from the *Unbridled* horses which gallop along the beach by the Santa Monica pier.

A stroll along the Venice Beach boardwalk takes you past the striking mural *Endangered Species*. Further along, gracing an alleyway at Windward and Speedway, *Venus Reconstituted* puts Boticelli's goddess on roller skates.

For more information and a tour of other murals around the city, contact the Social and Public Art Resource Center, which is located at 685 Venice Boulevard, tel. (310) 822-9560.

The **Third Street Promenade** is another of Santa Monica's popular shopping and dining areas. This three-block pedestrian mall, with its dinosaur topiaries, is delightful at any time of day but becomes especially lively on weekend evenings. From pubs to pool halls, and comedy clubs to poetry readings, the diversity of nightlife has made it one of the most popular places in L.A. Shops and cafés are open late, restaurants are generally inexpensive and street performers entertain the crowds.

Santa Monica has a large contingent of British residents, evident in the authentic pubs such as Ye Olde King's Head (complete with dart boards), just off the promenade, and the tea room at the Tudor House British Centre. Roughly 10-15 percent of the city's residents are of British descent, making up, perhaps, the largest British community outside the UK.

You're likely to spot a star or two in the chic boutiques along **Montana Avenue** (see p.93). Alternatively, you can head for the historic aircraft featured at Santa Monica Airport's **Museum of Flying**.

Just south of Rose Avenue, Main Street abruptly enters the bohemian community of **Venice Beach**. Ocean Front Walk is a magnet for the most outrageous characters in L.A., enacting their fantasies along a beach-side boardwalk that is lined with sidewalk artists, T-shirt vendors and Tarot readers. The show is at its best on the weekend afternoons, with everything from beach boys on unicycles to rock musicians on roller skates. The patch around 18th Avenue is known as Muscle Beach, where everyone oggles the body-builders who work out in the sand.

Thousands of pleasure boats dock at the vast man-made harbour of **Marina del Rey**. Harbour cruises and fishing trips can be arranged. Fisherman's Village on Fiji Way is a collection of gift shops and cafés styled like a New England seaport town. If you just want to watch the boats, you should be able to find a shady spot along Mindinao Way at Burton Chase Park.

PALOS VERDES TO SAN PEDRO

The coastal bluffs of the Palos Verdes Peninsula offer some of the loveliest views of the ocean, which can best be enjoyed from the winding Palos Verdes Drive. The **Point Vicente Lighthouse** with its adjacent **Interpretive Center** is a good stopping place at which to stretch your legs and admire the rugged beauty of the region. It's also a prime spot for whale-watching during their winter migration.

You'll find the pretty **Wayfarer's Chapel** sitting on the top of the southern cliffs. This intriguing glass structure, nestling amidst the trees, was created by Frank Lloyd Wright's son, and is a memorial to the Swedish philosopher Emanuel Swedenborg. It is open daily for meditation.

Amidst a bevy of beach towns, **San Pedro** is a working seaport which borders Los Angeles Harbor, the largest man-made port in the world. The shipyards stretch for miles and are most impressive from the top of the soaring arch of the Vincent Thomas Bridge. From here, you can watch the giant cranes as they unload the cargo ships from **Ports O'Call Village**, another twee, Cape Cod-style shopping centre for the tourist trade. You can also take harbour cruises from here.

*T*he unusual hilltop Wayfarer's Chapel provides beautiful views and a quiet retreat for travellers.

Hotels and Restaurants in Los Angeles

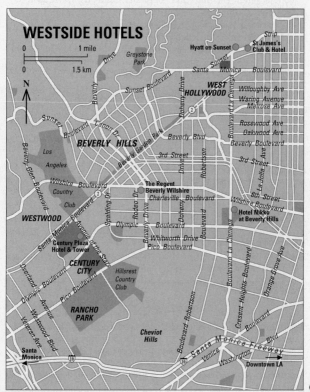

WESTSIDE HOTELS

0 — 1 mile
0 — 1.5 km

N

Greystone Park

Hyatt on Sunset

Strip
St James's Club & Hotel

Santa Monica Boulevard

WEST HOLLYWOOD

Sunset Boulevard

Willoughby Ave
Waring Avenue
Melrose Ave

Canon Dr

Rosewood Ave
Oakwood Ave
Beverly Boulevard

Beverly Drive

BEVERLY HILLS

Beverly Garden Park

Beverly Blvd

3rd Street

3rd Street

Dohany Drive

Boulevard La Cienega

Los Angeles

Wilshire Boulevard

Robertson

Beverly Glen Boulevard

Sunset Boulevard

La Jolla Ave

Country Club

WESTWOOD

Spalding Dr

The Regent Beverly Wilshire

Charleville Boulevard

6th Street

Wilshire Boulevard

Hotel Nikko at Beverly Hills

Santa Monica Boulevard

Avenue of the Stars

Rodeo Dr

Olympic

Beverly Drive

Dohany Drive

Boulevard

Whitworth Drive

Century Plaza Hotel & Tower

Pico Boulevard

Boulevard

Boulevard La Cienega

CENTURY CITY

Hillsrest Country Club

RANCHO PARK

Overland Boulevard

Olympic Boulevard

Pico Boulevard

Cheviot Hills

Santa Monica Freeway

Boulevard Robertson

Crescent Heights Boulevard

Orange Grove Ave

Westwood Blvd

Veteran Ave

Santa Monica

Venice

Washington

Blvd

Downtown LA

65

Recommended Hotels

The following hotels are listed alphabetically in three price categories, grouped according to regions within Los Angeles and Orange County. All hotels are of a high standard; most have king- or queen-sized beds and rooms include private bath, air-conditioning, television and telephone. Breakfast is not usually included at US hotels, except on executive floors, and at some budget motels which offer coffee and doughnuts.

For making direct reservations with the hotel, we have included telephone and, wherever possible, fax numbers. Check-out time is generally noon or 1pm, with check-in available from 2 to 3pm. All hotels accept major credit cards.

Prices vary greatly according to season, and many hotels offer special weekend packages and promotions during the year that are good value. Ask about such discounts when booking. As a basic guide to room prices, we have used the following symbols (two persons in a double room, per night):

III	$200 and up
II	$100-$200
I	under $100

DOWNTOWN

Checkers Hotel Kempinski II-III

535 South Grand Avenue
Los Angeles, CA 90071
Tel. (213) 624-0000
Toll-free 1-800-628-4900
Fax: (213) 626-9906
Small, historic, deluxe hotel with elegantly appointed rooms of antiques and fine artwork. Gourmet restaurants (see p.72) and lobby bar, rooftop pool and jacuzzi. 190 guest rooms, 17 suites.

Hotel InterContinental II-III

251 South Olive Street
Los Angeles, CA 90012-3002
Tel. (213) 617-3300
Fax: (213) 617-3399
Downtown's newest hotel, next to MOCA and the Watercourt. Public areas are decorated with modern artworks and sculpture, and the spacious rooms are in contemporary design. Lounge, two restaurants (see p.72), executive floor, health club, pool, and saunas. 439 guestrooms, 18 suites.

Hyatt Regency Los Angeles II-III

711 South Hope Street
Los Angeles, CA 90017
Tel. (213) 683-1234
Toll-free 1-800-233-1234
Fax: (213) 612-3179

Lovely atrium lobby with a crystal chandelier, and an adjacent shopping mall. Handsome rooms with marble bathrooms and views of the city. Fitness centre and spa, two restaurants, executive floor and Japanese services. 485 rooms, 41 luxury suites and 33 rooms for women business travellers.

Westin Bonaventure Hotel II

404 South Figueroa Street
Los Angeles, CA 90071
Tel. (213) 624-1000
Toll-free 1-800-228-3000
Fax: (213) 612-4894

This landmark hotel is a city-within-a-city, with a shopping gallery, 20 restaurants, five lounges and numerous services. The futuristic design features mirrored cylindrical towers around an open atrium lobby, which is adorned with reflecting pools. Rooms and glass-walled elevators give spectacular city vistas. Comfortable rooms, fine furnishings. Outdoor pool, executive floor and health club use. 1,474 guest rooms, 66 suites.

HOLLYWOOD

Radisson Hollywood Roosevelt Hotel I-III

7000 Hollywood Boulevard
Hollywood, CA 90028
Tel. (213) 466-7000
Toll-free 1-800-333-3333
Fax: (213) 462-8056

Historic hotel with classic, Spanish revival décor and movie star memorabilia. Courtyard, hot tub, pool, restaurant, cocktail lounge, and entertainment in the Cinegrill. 335 rooms, 35 luxury suites.

WESTSIDE

Century Plaza Hotel and Tower II-III

2025 Avenue of the Stars
Los Angeles, CA 90067
Tel. (310) 277-2000
Toll-free 1-800-228-3000
Fax: (310) 551-3355

Large, luxurious hotel with a tropical garden, overlooking the Schubert Theater. Rooms and suites are both spacious with marble baths and fine furniture; public areas are decorated with artworks. Three restaurants, three cocktail lounges, pool, jacuzzi, fitness centre, health club and tennis privileges, business centre, shops. 750 rooms and suites in the hotel, and 322 rooms and suites in the Tower.

67

Hotel Nikko at Beverly Hills IIII

465 South La Cienega Boulevard
Los Angeles, CA 90048
Tel. (310) 247-0400
Toll-free 1-800 -NIKKO-BH
Fax: (310) 246-2165

This luxury hotel caters to business travellers by providing high-tech amenities such as in-room fax and CD players and tranquil Japanese design. Restaurant, lounge, health club, sauna, pool, Japanese garden. 304 rooms, 42 suites.

Hyatt on Sunset II

8401 Sunset Boulevard
West Hollywood, CA 90069
Tel. (213) 656-1234
Toll-free 1-800 -233-1234
Fax: (213) 650-7024

In the Hollywood Hills and famous as the residence of rock stars playing the Sunset Strip. Rooftop swimming pool with great views, restaurant, sports bar and business centre. 262 rooms and suites.

The Regent Beverly Wilshire IIII

9500 Wilshire Boulevard
Beverly Hills, CA 90212
Tel. (310) 275-5200
Toll-free 1-800 -545-4000
Fax: (310) 205-0970

Grand, historic hotel at Wilshire Boulevard and Rodeo Drive. Elegant lobby with marble floors and columns and a crystal chandelier. The sumptuous rooms have plush furnishings and luxurious marble baths; Beverly Wing has balconies overlooking the pool. Pool, fitness centre and spa with steam room and sauna, three restaurants, bar, shops. 102 rooms, 44 suites.

St James Club & Hotel II-III

8358 Sunset Boulevard
Los Angeles, CA 90069
Tel. (213) 654-7100
Toll-free 1-800 -225-2637
Fax: (213) 654-9287

Luxurious, historic hotel furnished with replicas of Art Deco museum pieces from Paris and New York. Pool and terrace with city views, health centre, sauna, library, restaurant, bar and lounge. 63 rooms and suites, all with gondola beds and exquisite baths.

SAN FERNANDO VALLEY

Holiday Inn Burbank II

150 East Angeleno
Burbank, CA 91502
Tel. (818) 841-4770
Toll-free 1-800 -HOLIDAY
Fax: (818) 566-7886

Towers, one with 102 two-room suites. Restaurant, pool, sauna.